Contents

Uses of Materials

Science putty

Science putty is very soft and stretchy. A small blob can be stretched a long way before it snaps!

Science putty becomes brittle if you put it in the freezer. It can be smashed by hitting it with a hammer!

Science putty can move on its own! If you leave a blob of it on the floor, it goes flat to make a puddle!

Thermochromic materials

Thermochromic materials change colour very quickly when the temperature changes.

They can be used for fun things!

This rubber duck changes colour when you put it into a hot bath!

This t-shirt changes colour when you touch it!

They are sometimes used for serious reasons too.

This thermometer changes colour if a baby's bath water is too hot.

Things to do

List things that you think could be made out of these marvellous materials in the future.

Record it!

Scientists record the results of their investigations in lots of different ways.

This scientist has been investigating the breaking strength of different types of materials but can't decide which is the best way to show what happened.

Scientists use Newton meters to measure breaking strength. You can too!

The question the scientist has been asked is: How much force does it take to break different materials?

Here are four possible ways the results could be recorded. Which way of recording results do you think is the best? Why?

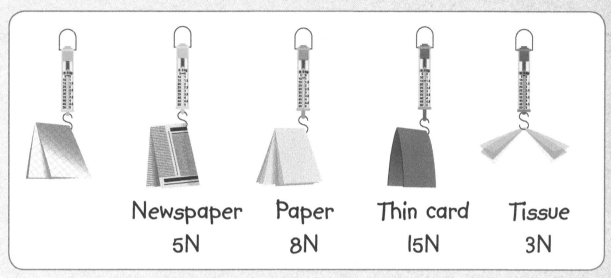

Newspaper 5N   Paper 8N   Thin card 15N   Tissue 3N

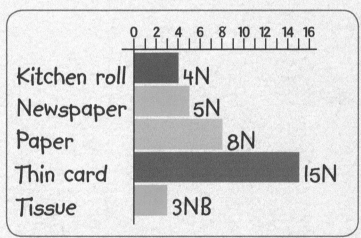

| 0 2 4 6 8 10 12 14 16 |
Kitchen roll	4N
Newspaper	5N
Paper	8N
Thin card	15N
Tissue	3NB

Materials	Force
Kitchen roll	4N
Newspaper	5N
Paper	8N
Thin card	15N
Tissue	3N

Kitchen roll 4N
Newspaper 5N
Paper 8N
Thin card 15N
Tissue 3N

Uses of Materials

Precious materials

Some materials are very expensive to buy. They are often used to make jewellery.

Most of these materials are natural and need to be dug out of the ground by miners.

They then need to be polished and shaped to make the jewellery.

Find out

Find out about other precious materials used in making jewellery. Where do they come from? How many can you list?

Things to do

Mining can be very dangerous. Mining can also be very exciting! Would you like to be a miner one day?

Living Things

Alive or not alive?
What makes something alive?

Which of these things are alive?

How can you tell?

That's my mummy

Some living things look like their parents from birth. Others look very different. Sometimes even the names of the living things change when they grow up!

a baby and a woman

a kitten and a cat

a cygnet and a swan

some frogspawn and a frog

an acorn and an oak tree

a bulb and a plant

some seeds and a plant

How are these parents different from their babies?

Find out

What do these animals grow up to be?

- Fawn
- Squab
- Leveret

Find out

How many types of animal babies are called pups?

Match the pairs!

Look at the pictures. Can you find the babies and what they grow up to be?

Growing Plants

Seeds

Seeds come in all shapes and sizes. If they have everything they need, seeds will grow into new plants. Most plants grow from seeds. Some plants grow from bulbs. A bulb isn't a real seed.

Can you guess which plant each seed grows into? Do the biggest seeds grow into the biggest plants? Which plant comes from the bulb?

Seeds need ...

Seeds are found all over the world, but they all need light, air and water to grow.

Did you know?

Peach seeds contain poison called cyanide. So don´t eat that bit!

Did you know?

A single dandelion flower head has about 200 seeds in it!

The Millennium Seed Bank

There is a seed bank in Sussex, England. It stores millions of seeds from all around the world. If a plant ever died out in nature, seeds from the bank could be grown to replace it.

Did you know?

The oldest seed ever to be grown into a plant was a date palm seed from Israel. It was 2500 years old, but it still grew!

The Millennium Seed Bank is the world's largest seed bank.

What seeds would you save for the future?

Seeds you can eat

Three seeds are very important for feeding people all around the world. They are rice, maize and wheat.

We can boil rice and eat it.

We can use maize to make popcorn!

We can use wheat to make bread.

Investigate it!

Some children are investigating what makes plants grow well. They have some questions. Match the questions to the investigations in the pictures.

Do plants grow better in the light or the dark?

Do plants need water to grow well?

Do plants grow better in warm or cool places?

Things to do

Think of another question to investigate.

Changing Shape

Bending, twisting, squashing, stretching!

Some materials change shape easily.
Some materials don't seem to change at all.

We can change the shape of materials by bending them, twisting them, squashing them and stretching them.

Things to do

Make a list of all the materials you have touched today. Which materials change shape easily? Which materials do not?

Rubber

Rubber is an amazing material! You can squash it, bend it, stretch it, twist it and bounce it. But where does it come from? Believe it or not, rubber comes from trees!

The white liquid from rubber trees was used to make shoes.

Rubber was first discovered hundreds of years ago by people living in Central and South America. They collected the white liquid that oozed from the rubber trees and smeared it onto their feet to make shoes.

The white liquid collected from rubber trees is called latex.

Did you know?

Rubber trees are difficult to find, so scientists have developed a way to make rubber in their labs.

Rubber safety tiles are used in playgrounds.

Rubber is used to make wellies!

Things to do

Rubber is still used today to make thousands of things. How many can you think of?

Changing Shape

Rope twisting

A rope is made by twisting long, stringy materials together.

The first ever ropes were made by twisting vines together.

The Ancient Egyptians made special tools to help them make rope. These tools held one end of the rope so that the rope maker could use both hands to twist.

Egyptians used special tools to make rope from plant fibres.

Things to do
Make your own rope by twisting pieces of string together.

Predict it!

Rulers are made from different materials and can be different sizes.

Find some different rulers.

Look at the rulers. Which one do you think is the most bendy?

Put the rulers in order from most bendy to least bendy.

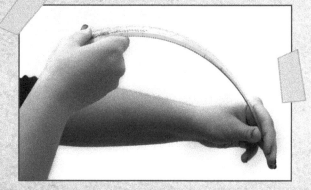

Test the rulers.

Were you right?

Feeding and Exercise

Where does my meal come from?

Many of us buy our food from shops and supermarkets. Where does this food originally come from?

All food comes from either plants or animals.

Which of these foods come from plants? Which come from animals? Which are mixtures of both?

Food needs to be farmed, caught or grown. Can you think of examples of each?

From farm to fork

Food often needs to be changed in some way before we eat it. Look at these pictures. How has the food been changed?

Who eats who?
All animals need to eat to live. Food gives us energy to live and grow.

A food chain shows how each living thing gets its energy. Food chains begin with plants. Plants get energy from the Sun. Food chains end with animals. Some animals eat plants, some eat other animals.

Here is a food chain from the rainforest.

green rainforest plants   agouti   jaguar

Here is a food chain from the desert.

desert cacti   kangaroo rat   hawk

Can you think of a food chain for where you live?

Did you know?

Humans are at the end of many food chains. We can choose to eat plants or animals or both.

Science Skills

Plan it!

Class Two are investigating which food birds prefer. They have four types of food.

 mealworms

 bread

 fruit

 seeds

The children cannot decide how to do the investigation. Can you help them?

We should weigh all the food and keep the mass the same.

We should keep the volume of the food the same because the bread is lighter than the fruit.

We only have three containers. Does that matter?

Does it matter what time of day we do the test?

Habitats

Who lives where?
Would a whale survive in a wood?
What about in a river?

Would a tree
survive under
the sea?

All living things have their own special place to live. We call this place a habitat.

My home, my habitat

A habitat is a place in the natural world where plants and animals live. A habitat provides food and shelter. It is a place where living things feel safe and can produce offspring.

Find out

Who lives in habitats like these?

Did you know?

Humans can live in most habitats because, unlike animals, we wear clothes and build shelters to help us survive.

Small is beautiful

Some habitats, like the ocean, are large. Other habitats, like underneath a log, are very small. All habitats give animals and plants the things they need. We call very small habitats 'micro-habitats'.

a micro-habitat

Minibeast mission

Look for micro-habitats in your school grounds. Can you find any of these living things?

earthworm

daisy

spider

wasp

ladybird

woodlouse

earwig

ant

snail

lichen

Did you know?

'Centipede' means 'a hundred legs', but most centipedes only have 30 legs!

Sometimes we may not see the animal, but we can see where it lives.

Find out

Find out about 'extremophiles'. These are animals who live in hostile habitats.

Did you know?

Dragonflies have been on Earth since before the dinosaurs!

Index